Weevils

This book has been reviewed
for accuracy by
Walter L. Gojmerac
Professor of Entomology
University of Wisconsin—Madison.

Library of Congress Cataloging in Publication Data

Heymann, Georgianne.
  Weevils.

  (Nature close-ups)
  Adaptation of: Zōmushi / Oda Hidetomo.
  Summary: Discusses the life cycles and habitats
of various kinds of weevils.
  1. Beetles—Juvenile literature. [1. Beetles]
I. Oda, Hidetomo. Zōmushi. II. Title. III. Series.
QL576.2.H49 1986   595.76′8   86-26240
ISBN 0-8172-2713-X (lib. bdg.)
ISBN 0-8172-2731-8 (softcover)

This edition first published in 1987 by Raintree Publishers Inc.

Text copyright © 1987 by Raintree Publishers Inc., translated by
Jun Amano from *Weevils* copyright © 1983 by Hidetomo Oda.

Photographs copyright © 1983 by Hidekazu Kubo.

World English translation rights for *Color Photo Books on Nature*
arranged with Kaisei-Sha through Japan Foreign-Rights Center.

1 2 3 4 5 6 7 8 9 0   90 89 88 87 86

Weevils

Adapted by
Georgianne Heymann

Raintree Publishers
Milwaukee

◀ **A weevil cutting a stalk.**

The front part of this weevil's head is shaped into a long nose-like beak, or snout. Strong jaws and sharp teeth are at the end of its snout.

▶ **A weevil on a raspberry stalk.**

Some weevils eat the fruit or seeds of plants, others eat the stems, leaves, or roots.

In spring, when the green shoots of new plants poke through the ground and flowers open, many weevils begin to leave their winter homes. The coming of spring is the sign that there will be food for the hungry weevils that have rested through the winter. Although the weevil is very small, sometimes so small it is hard to see, it is one of the most harmful of insects.

Both adult and young weevils feed on plants. There are more than forty thousand different kinds of weevils, and each kind has certain plants that it likes to feed on. Each year these plant-feeding insects cause millions of dollars of damage when they eat crops that farmers grow and store. Whole crops can be destroyed by the weevil. Sometimes farmers spray chemicals called insecticides over their crops to kill insects. When there is no way to protect the crop from weevils, farmers are forced to raise animals or grow a crop that weevils do not eat.

◀ **Raspberries.**

▶ **Cutting a leaf from a raspberry stalk.**

With its strong-toothed jaws, called mandibles, the weevil is able to chew through the tough plant stem, causing the leaves of the raspberry stalk to fall off.

▲ **A female chewing a hole in a plant stem.**

Before laying her eggs, the female chews deep holes in a plant stem.

▲ **A weevil laying an egg.**

After the cavity is ready, the female places her ovipositor into the hole and lays an egg.

Weevils also lay their eggs in plants. Each kind, or species, of weevil has special plants that it searches for when it wants to lay its eggs. Some weevils lay their eggs in the stalks or stems of plants, others deposit their eggs in the flowers or the fruits of certain plants.

Each group of weevils lays its eggs in a special way. Some weevils cut through the stalk and stop sap from reaching part of the plant. Without sap, the part quickly dies. Then the weevil uses its long snout, with its sharp teeth and strong jaws, to chew deep holes in the dead, dried out part of the plant. Other weevils make a place for their eggs without killing any part of the plant.

Once the hole, or cavity, is made, the female weevil extends a long tube, called an ovipositor, from the back part of her body into the hole. The egg travels through the ovipositor into the cavity.

◀ **Ripe raspberries and a withering stalk.**

Ripe summer berries attract some species of weevils to the raspberry plant (left photo). Cut away from the stalk, the raspberry branch quickly begins to dry out (right photo).

▼ **Inside a raspberry stalk.**

An egg has been placed in the largest of the three holes in the stalk.

▼ **Hiding the egg.**

Before leaving the stalk, the female chews up pieces of the plant and stuffs them into the opening of the cavity.

◄ A withered raspberry stalk.

The stalk with the weevil nest has become dried out and hard. The black arrow points to the eggs within the stalk.

▶ The developing larva inside the egg (photos 1-3).

Beneath the surface of the egg, the head and body of the larva can be seen forming. Soon after the jaws become brown, the larva will emerge.

Within the withered stalk, the weevil egg is safe from animals, called predators, that hunt it for food. Besides being a protective home for the egg, the stalk surrounding the egg supplies food for the weevil as it grows.

The physical changing from an egg to an adult weevil is called a metamorphosis. All insects go through some kind of metamorphosis. Insects that change in three stages are said to go through an incomplete metamorphosis. Weevils have a complete metamorphosis because they go through four stages: egg, larva, pupa, and adult. With each stage, the weevil changes dramatically.

Inside the egg, the larva begins to form. In a matter of days, the brown head and white body of the larva can be seen beneath the surface of the egg. Soon the larva comes out of, emerges from, the egg. Its soft round body is without legs or wings. But its jaws are well formed, and the hungry larva immediately starts to feed.

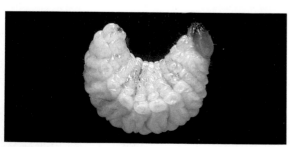

◄ The weevil larva.

The soft wormlike body of the larva has a hard brown head with strong jaws.

▶ A newly emerged larva.

The newly emerged larva does not need to search for food. It finds plenty to eat inside the plant stem.

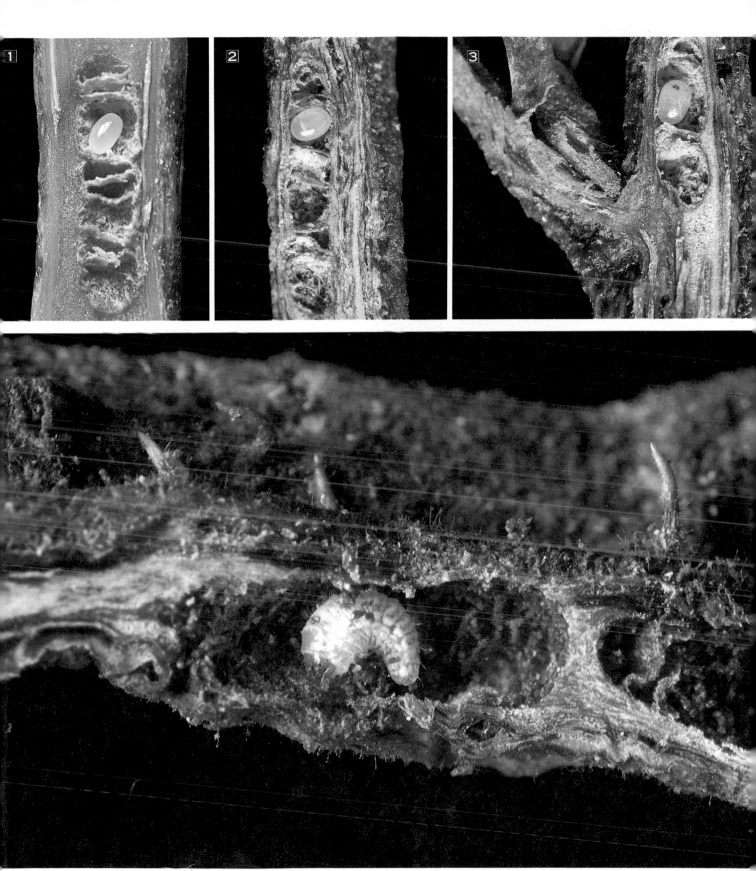

▲ **A tree weevil.**

This brightly colored weevil lives on oak trees during the summer. Its larvae live under the bark and make a network of tunnels as they feed.

▲ **A waterweed weevil.**

In summer, this brown weevil lays her eggs in weeds near lakes and rivers.

Although there are many different kinds of weevils, the eggs of most weevils look very much alike. If a stem with weevil eggs were opened, it would be impossible to tell what the adult weevils would eventually look like. Each species of adult weevil looks different. Some have slender smooth bodies, others have fat bumpy bodies. There are spotted weevils, and striped weevils. All weevils belong to the same large family, the Curculionidae family.

All the members of the weevil family look alike in some ways. The front part of the head is shaped into a nose-like beak, or snout. Sometimes the snout is as long as the body. Antennae come off the sides of the snout and bend, like elbows. The weevil uses its antennae to smell and touch objects. The antennae, which are thickened like little clubs at the end, can be folded back alongside the snout when the weevil is feeding.

● **A spotted weevil.**

Most weevils, like this spotted one, belong to the group of weevils with long downward curving snouts called true weevils (right). The spotted weevil lays her eggs near the roots of dayflowers (left).

▼ An egg laid inside a plant stalk. A weevil chewed this plant stalk to make a hole for its egg (left). Most weevils lay small white eggs (right).

◀ **A field of arrowroots.**

On a summer day, a growing field of arrowroots is an active feeding ground (upper photo). Following a rain, *Mesalcidodes trifidus* clings to a slippery arrowroot stalk (lower photo).

▶ **Feeding on an arrowroot stalk.**

As it moves down the arrowroot stalk, the weevil uses its curved snout to eat a deep channel in the stalk.

There are so many species of weevils that many do not have a common name. They are known only by their scientific name. *Mesalcidodes trifidus* is the scientific name of the black and white weevil on these pages.

This black and white weevil is feeding on arrowroot stalks, but it also eats other plants. Most weevils feed on more than one kind of plant, but there may be one plant that it prefers. When a species of weevil—such as the boll weevil—feeds and lays its eggs on just one kind of plant, it can do great harm to those plants. Plants are left with spoiled fruits, dried and brown stalks, and chewed leaves. However, not all plants die when weevils feed on them. Sometimes the plant can keep growing, and the damage that was done may even be repaired.

▶ **The fast recovery of an arrowroot.**

The channel made by the weevil can be seen in this view of the arrowroot stalk (left photo). Later, the plant has grown and some of the damage has been repaired (right photo).

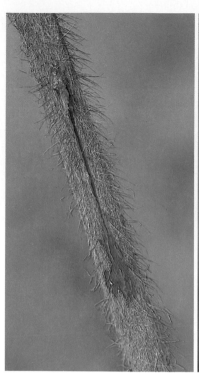
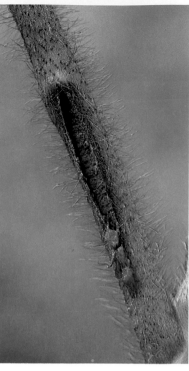

The everyday activities of weevils change when male and female weevils mate. Usually, the black and white arrowroot weevil digs a straight groove in the arrowroot stalk when it is feeding. But when the female is ready to mate, she walks around and around the stalk, digging a spiral groove. The spiral groove will be the nest for her eggs. When the male weevil sees the female making the spiral nest, he is attracted to her.

Some weevils make sounds when they are being attacked. A squeaking sound is made when a "file" on the weevil's abdomen is rubbed by a "scraper" on the wing. The same sound is used to help some male and female weevils find each other when it is time to mate.

When the male finally finds the female, he climbs onto her back. During mating, the male passes sperm through a hardened tube at the end of his abdomen into the female. The female keeps the sperm in a baglike part of her abdomen. Before the eggs are laid, they are united with the sperm, or fertilized.

▲ **Preparing a place to deposit an egg.**

As she digs a spiral groove, the female weevil stops from time to time to make deep holes in the groove for her eggs.

▲ **Laying an egg.**

When the hole is deep enough, the female places her ovipositor into it and lays an egg.

The number of eggs that the female weevil lays depends on the species. Climate can also make a difference. Weevils in warm climates may lay eggs constantly during their short lives. Insects in cooler areas go through fewer generations.

After laying the eggs, the female weevil does not stay to care for them. So it is important that the place where the eggs are laid will be a good food supply for the develop-ing weevils. It must also be well protected from predators. Many insects, including other weevils, feed on the eggs.

Some species hide their eggs by digging deep holes and covering the openings with chewed-up pieces of the plant. Others secrete a sticky fluid, called mucus, and seal the opening to the nest. Still others bury their dark eggs in the ground where the color makes the eggs hard to find.

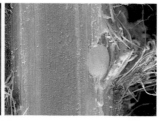

◀ **An egg inside the stalk.**

The small white egg is held to the stalk by a sticky fluid the female secretes (left photo). When the stalk is cut open, the egg can be seen in the hole deep within the stalk (right photo).

▼ **Weevil eggs hidden inside a plant stalk.**

Although a winding groove can be seen on the outside of the stalk, the eggs are hidden by the thick plant growth.

▼ **A stalk with many eggs.**

When the surface of the stalk is peeled away, the eggs can be seen in the spiral grooves.

▲ **A newly emerged larva.**

A hungry larva crawls out of the egg and immediately eats the empty egg shell.

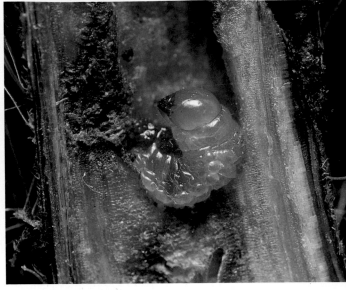

▲ **The changing larva.**

Shortly after emerging, the larva's skin begins to darken. Soon it is no longer transparent.

After emerging from the egg, the larva spends its life inside its food supply eating and growing. Usually weevil larvae live much longer than the adults. Some may spend as long as three or four years as larvae. During that time, they rest, or hibernate, through the winter. Because larvae live so long and eat so much, they can do a lot of damage to plants at this stage.

The larva grows rapidly, but its skin does not stretch enough for its body. When the skin becomes too tight, it splits and the larva crawls out. A new skin forms and hardens. The new skin will also become too small, and the larva will again shed its skin, or molt.

◄ **A stalk with eggs.**

The grooved surface of the arrowroot stalk becomes dry and brown (left photo). As the plant grows, the stalk thickens around the nest site (right photo).

▼ The growing stalk.

The stalk continues to grow around the larvae inside. As the larvae grow, the stalk becomes knotted and lumpy, forming a gall.

▼ Inside the stalk.

Each larva is in a small room, or chamber, with walls made from its own waste.

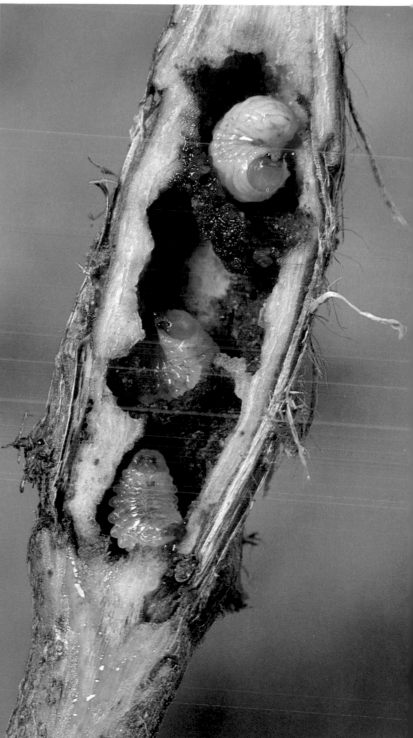

◄ An arrowroot knot.

By the time the larvae are full grown, the gall has grown very large. A gall can reach three inches in length and an inch in width.

► The arrowroot in bloom.

When the arrowroot blooms, the stalk and leaves stop growing. Inside the stalk, the larvae are ready to pupate.

Most weevils molt three times before the larvae are fully grown. But some molt as many as fifteen times. The stage between moltings is called an instar. With each instar, the larva continues to eat, making a larger chamber for itself. The waste material the larva adds to its nest helps to strengthen the walls of the chamber. The chamber forms a hard, knotty bump on the plant. It is called a gall.

After the last molting, the larva stops eating and becomes immobile inside the gall. Many changes take place as the pupa forms under the larva's final skin. Soon the skin splits, and the pupa emerges, looking like a small white mummy with an elephant's trunk.

▼ A full-grown larva.

The larva has completed its growth and rests in the pupal chamber.

▼ Inside the pupal chamber.

The pupa emerges from the larval skin looking like a small pale mummy.

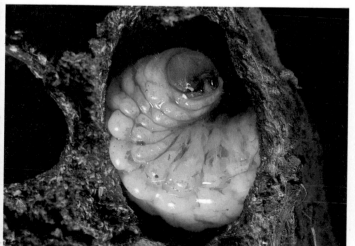

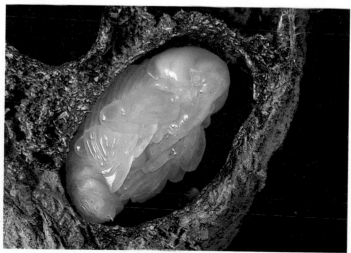

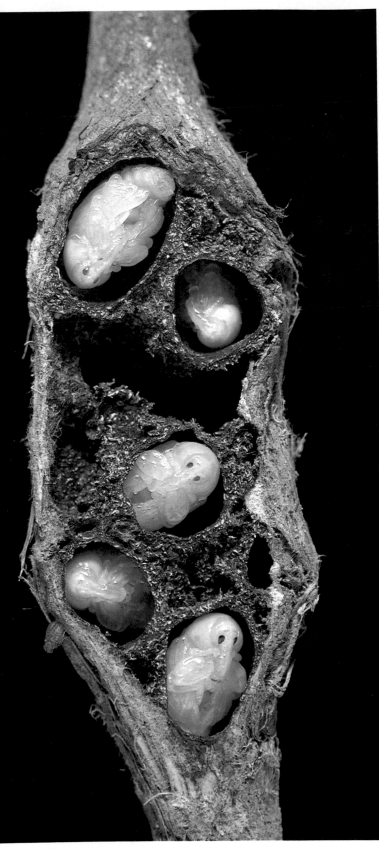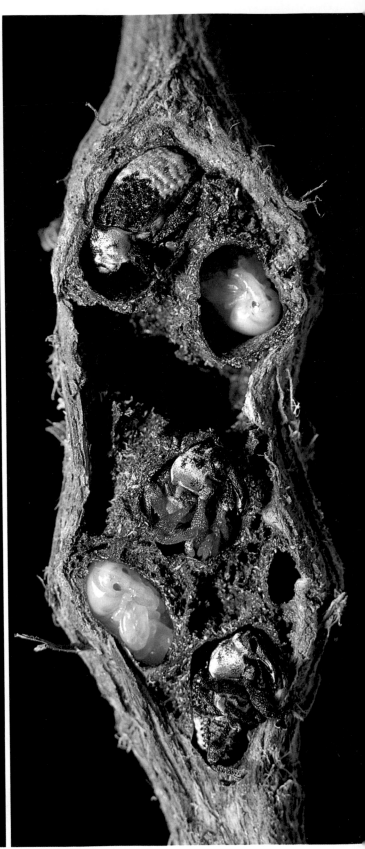

◄ Pupae and adult weevils.

As the pupae develop, their eyes become darker (left photo). The nest is filled with weevils in different stages of growth (right photo).

► An adult weevil emerging.

At the end of summer, the adult weevil bites its way through the gall to the outside.

Inside the pupal shell, new parts are being formed. Antennae appear, eyes darken, legs and wings develop. Through the transparent pupal skin, the pupa looks more and more like the adult weevil. Finally, the pupa is fully developed. The pupa's skin splits open. It is the last molt of the weevil, and the full-grown adult emerges to begin the final stage of its life cycle.

The body of the new adult weevil is soft and lightly colored. The weevil waits in its chamber for the outer skin to darken and harden. The wings, which were folded close to the weevil's body, slowly stretch out to full size. The front wings, called elytra, are thick and hard. The elytra cover and protect the rear flying wings when they are not in use.

Soon the weevil is ready to come out of its pupal chamber. After leaving, it will look for food and then a mate to start a new generation of weevils.

▼ The new adult weevil.

At first the newly emerged weevil's body is soft and lightly colored.

▼ Folding its wings.

The darkened weevil stretches out its thin back wings, then folds them under its front wings and waits while its body hardens and dries.

◄ **A nut weevil on an acorn.**

Nut weevils have long, slender snouts. Their muted brown color, much like the bark of trees, keeps them hidden from their enemies.

► **Nut weevils mating on a chestnut burr.**

Another very different looking group of weevils are the nut weevils. They have needle-like snouts almost as long as their bodies. Like all other weevils, they have strong jaws and well-developed mouthparts at the end of their snouts.

Among the nut weevils are the *Curculio arakawai* that feed on acorns. After these acorn weevils mate in late summer, the female lays her eggs inside growing acorns.

▼ **A weevil preparing a place to lay her eggs.**

To make a cavity, the nut weevil digs through the hard top of the acorn to the soft fleshy part of the nut.

▼ **A weevil laying an egg.**

After the hole is made, the nut weevil pokes her ovipositor into the hole and lays her eggs. The ovipositor is almost as long as her snout.

▲ **A female laying an egg in a chestnut.**

Many female nut weevils chew holes in which to lay their eggs, in either chestnuts or acorns.

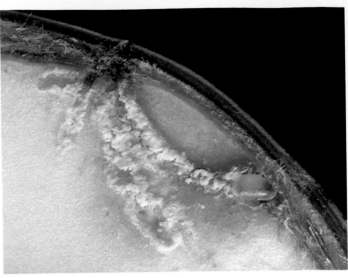

▲ **An egg laid in a chestnut.**

A small egg has been laid at the end of one of the holes in a chestnut. The other holes were made by nut weevils feeding.

The female acorn weevil drills through the hard outer shell of the nut to make small chambers for her eggs. She lays one egg in each chamber and seals the opening to the chamber with a ball of waste material. The larva emerges from the egg and develops as other larvae, feeding and molting in its nest.

Although some plants recover and keep on growing after weevil larvae have nested in them, acorns are destroyed by the nut larvae. Because the acorn is the seed of oak trees, the growth of oak forests can be severely threatened when the nut weevil nests in acorns.

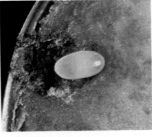

◄ **A gray female weevil laying an egg.**

During early fall, the gray weevil lays her eggs (left photo). Although the gray weevil doesn't have the needle-like snout of many nut weevils, she still is able to dig through the tough nut surface and make a cavity for her egg inside an acorn (right photo).

▼ **A larva feeding on a chestnut.** A young larva feeds on a chestnut and leaves behind a pile of white powdery waste (left). When the larva is older and larger, it leaves behind heavy black and brown waste (right).

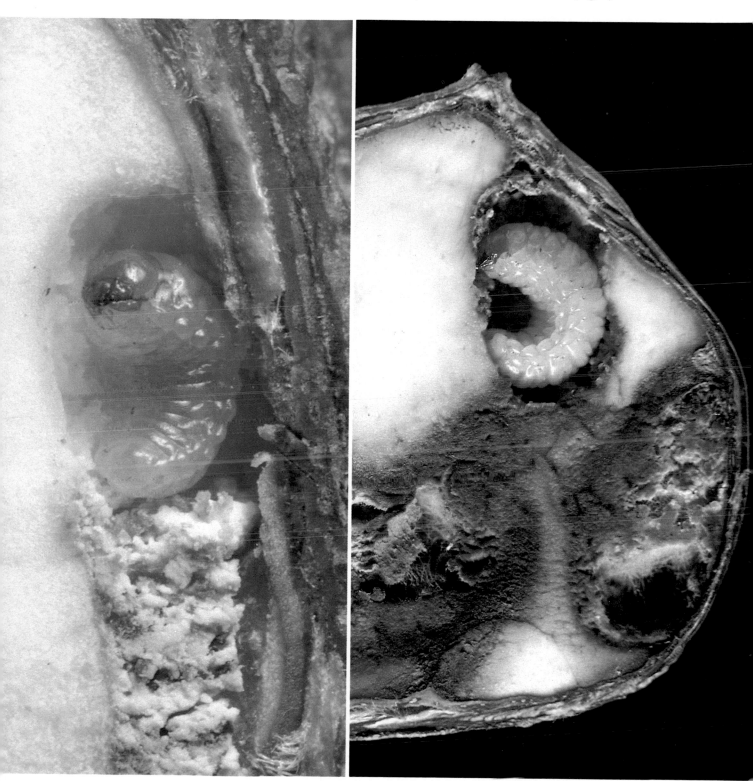

◀ **A larva coming out of a chestnut.**

In late fall, a nut weevil makes its way out of a fallen chestnut. It bites through the hard outer shell. When the hole is big enough, it pokes its head through the shell. Slowly it squeezes its fat body through the hole to the outside.

▶ **Nut weevils make their nests in nuts like these large green chestnut burrs.**

By the time the nut ripens and drops to the ground, the nut larva is fully grown. The larva uses its strong jaws to chew its way out of the nut. Then the larva burrows into the soil. Once beneath the ground, it presses its body against the ground to form a neat round chamber for itself. The chamber will be its winter home.

Rather than immediately beginning the pupal stage, most nut weevil larvae hibernate during the winter. Some even spend more than one winter as a larva, hibernating. As spring approaches, the nut weevil larvae pupate. In summer, the adult weevil emerges from its winter chamber to look for a mate.

▼ **A hibernating larva.**

The resting larva will spend the winter underground in its round pupal chamber.

▼ **A newly emerged pupa.**

The pupa has shed its larval skin. Inside the pupal skin, the adult nut weevil is forming.

Let's Find Out How to Raise Weevils.

(1) A weevil's long snout. (2) An egg on an arrowroot stalk. (3) A weevil larva growing in a dried raspberry stalk. (4) A large weevil eating tree sap. This weevil may grow to be an inch long. (5) Weevils on an arrowroot leaf.

Adult weevils use their long snouts to chew holes in plant stems to lay their eggs. Look for small holes or bruises on plants where weevils used to live. You may be able to find weevil eggs hidden there. If you find some eggs, take them home and watch them hatch. Feed the larvae the same kind of plant on which the eggs were laid.

▲ An adult weevil feeding on a rice plant. ▲ A rice plant leaf eaten by a weevil.

◄ **Weevils that feed on rice.**

Both adult weevils and larvae feed on plants. Some species of weevils feed on farmers' crops. The adult weevil in this picture eats the leaves of rice plants. The larvae feed on the roots of rice plants.

Let's Check a Raspberry Stalk.

Look for a hole made by a weevil in a raspberry stalk. If you cut into the stalk, you may find a weevil egg. A dried, hardened stalk may contain a weevil larva.

▲ A weevil.   ▲ An egg in a stalk.

Let's Raise a Weevil.

If you find a weevil, keep it in a plastic bag. Feed it and watch carefully to see if it lays eggs. You may also find weevil eggs on other leaves on the plant.

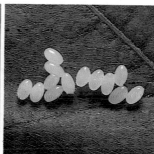

▲ A leaf with eggs.   ▲ Eggs.

Let's Look for Weevils That Live in Legumes.

There are several species of weevils that feed on peas, beans, clover, and other plants that are legumes. The weevils live on the legumes until they become adults.

▲ These photos show different kinds of weevils that eat legumes.

Let's Look for Nut Weevils.

Find a tree that has ripe nuts. Shake some branches with a stick to knock down nuts. You may find nut weevils in acorns, hazelnuts, walnuts, and perhaps in chestnuts. Open some nuts to see if there are weevil larvae inside.

▲ Acorns and a larva.   ▲ Chestnuts.

GLOSSARY

abdomen—the back, or rear section, of an insect's body. (p. 14)

antennae—the movable feelers on an insect's head that detect odor and movement. (pp. 10, 23)

elytra—the thick hard front wings of some beetles that cover and protect the thin membranous back wings used for flying. (p. 23)

fertilized—when a sperm and egg unite, making it possible for a new organism to form. (p. 14)

insecticide—a chemical or mixture of chemicals used for killing insects and other pests. (p. 4)

metamorphosis—a process of development during which physical changes take place. Complete metamorphosis involves four stages: egg, larva, pupa, and adult. Incomplete metamorphosis occurs in three stages: egg, nymph, and adult. (p. 8)

ovipositor—an egg-laying tube that extends from the tip of an insect's abdomen. (pp. 6, 16)

predator—an animal that hunts or kills other animals for food. (pp. 8, 16)

sap—the fluid in a plant that brings nourishment to all parts of the plant. (p. 6)

species—a group of animals that scientists have identified as having common traits. (pp. 6, 10, 13)